JOKES FOR KIDS:

The MEGA Laugh-out-Loud Joke Book for Kids

JENNY KELLETT

ISBN-13: 978-1519389268
ISBN-10: 1519389264

Contents

ONE-LINERS

Why did a frog eat a lamp?

Because he wanted a light snack!

• • • • •

What do you call James Bond in a bathtub?

Bubble-07!

What did the dentist give the marching band?

A tuba toothpaste!

• • • • •

What do witches put on their hair?

Scare spray!

• • • • •

Why did the banana peel?

It didn't have any suntan lotion on!

• • • • •

What kind of animals need oiling?

A mouse, because it squeaks!

• • • • •

Why did the girl tiptoe past the medicine cabinet?

Because she didn't want to wake the sleeping pills.

• • • • •

Why did the man put the rabbit on his head?

Because he had no hare!

• • • • •

How much money does a skunk have?

One scent!

• • • • •

Where are chicks born?

In Chick-cago!

• • • • •

Why didn't the mummy have any friends?

Because he was too wrapped up in himself!

• • • • •

Why did the witches call off the baseball game?

They couldn't find the bats.

• • • • •

What do you call a girl with a frog on her head?

Lily.

• • • • •

What do you call a penguin in the desert?

Lost!

• • • • •

What years do kangaroos like best?

Leap years!

• • • • •

What time is it when an elephant sits on your fence?

Time to get a new fence!

• • • • •

Why is it so hot after a baseball game?

Because all the fans have gone home.
• • • • •

Where do cows go on their holidays?

To BerMOOda!

• • • • •

Why was the ghost a cheerleader?

Because she liked to show off her school spirit.

• • • • •

What is a cow's favorite activity at school?

Moo-sic!

• • • • •

Why can't you tell a joke when you're on the ice?

Because it might crack up!

• • • • •

How do dogs turn off the VCR?

By hitting the paws button.

• • • • •

What is a dogs favorite color?

Grrrreen!

• • • • •

Why did the tightrope walker visit the bank?

He wanted to check his balance!

• • • • •

What happened to the glass blower who inhaled?

He got a pane in his stomach.

• • • • •

Where do you dance in California?

San Frandisco!

• • • • •

Why did the man dance in front of the bottle?

It said, 'twist to open'!

• • • • •

Why did the teacher get her eyes tested?

Because her pupils were acting crazy!

• • • • •

Why did the worker at the M&M factory get fired?

He threw all the W's away!

• • • • •

What is a shark's favorite game?

Swallow the leader!

• • • • •

What did the bunny say to the duck?

You quack me up!

• • • • •

When's the best time for trampolining?

Springtime!

• • • • •

What do garbagemen eat?

Junk food!

• • • • •

What's worse than finding a worm in your apple?

Finding HALF a worm in your apple!

• • • • •

How do you unlock a haunted house?

With a skeleton key!

• • • • •

What do cats like on hot dogs?

Mouse-stard.

• • • • •

Customer: Waiter, what's this fly doing in my soup?

Waiter: I think it's doing backstroke.

• • • • •

Which sport is always in trouble?

Bad-minton.

• • • • •

What do you call it when you cross a dinosaur and a pig?

Jurassic pork!

• • • • •

If two is company and three's a crowd, what are four and five?

Nine!

• • • • •

What do you call two witches who live together?

Broommates!

• • • • •

What is a centipede's favorite toy?

Leg-os!

• • • • •

How do you start a fire with two sticks?

Make sure one of the sticks is a match!

• • • • •

Why do you put band aids in the fridge?

For cold cuts!

• • • • •

What do you call a yak in the jungle?

Lost!

• • • • •

What has a bottom on its top?

Your leg!

• • • • •

How does a rose ride a bike?

By pushing its petals!

• • • • •

What do you call a cow that has no milk?

An udder failure!

• • • • •

What did the envelope say to the stamp?

Stick with me and we'll go places!

• • • • •

What kind of dog does Dracula want?

A bloodhound!

• • • • •

How do monsters like their eggs?

Terri-fried!

• • • • •

What do you do when there's a kidnapping?

Wake them up!

• • • • •

Why don't crows ever get hit by cars?

Because one is always in the tree yellowing 'caw, caw!'.

• • • • •

Who made King Arthur's round table?

Sir Cumference!

• • • • •

What did one shooting star say to the other?

Pleased to meteor!

• • • • •

What kind of wood is a king?

A ruler!

• • • • •

What did the raspberry say to the blueberry? I love you berry, berry much!

• • • • •

What does a cannibal call a phone book?

A menu!

Why did the monster put a keep off sign on her lawn?

She wanted to mark her terror-tory!

• • • • •

What do you call a bull that is afraid?

A cow-ard!

• • • • •

What do you call a bird in the freezer?

A birrrrrd!

• • • • •

What do birds wear to the beach?

Beak-inis!

• • • • •

Why did the boy say moo?

Because he was a cowboy!

• • • • •

How many witches does it take to change a light bulb?

Just one, but she changes it into a frog.

• • • • •

Why was the chicken sick?

Because it had people pox!

• • • • •

In which country do people's tummies rumble most?

Hungary!

• • • • •

What brand of underwear does King Tut wear?

Fruit of the tomb!

• • • • •

How did the farmer count his cows?

With a cowculator!

• • • • •

Where do most ants live?

In Antlantic City!

• • • • •

What did Obi-Wan say to Anakin at lunch?

Use the forks, Anakin!

• • • • •

What do you call a dancing sheep?

A baa-lerina.

• • • • •

What do computers like to eat?

Chips!

• • • • •

What kind of wood is a king?

A ruler!

• • • • •

What did the raspberry say to the blueberry?

I love you berry, berry much!

• • • • •

What does a cannibal call a phone book?

A menu!

• • • • •

Why was the clock sent to the principal's office?

Because he was tocking too much!

• • • • •

What happened to the cat who ate a ball of yarn?

She had mittens.

• • • • •

What do you call an underwater spy?

James Pond!

• • • • •

Why did the snake cross the road?

To get to the other s-s-s-side!

• • • • •

What is 1,500 miles long, 24 centuries old, and purple?

The Grape Wall of China.

• • • • •

What do you get when you cross a dinosaur with a pig?

Jurassic Pork!

• • • • •

What do boxers and astronomers have in common?

They both see stars!

• • • • •

What's the best way to call a T-Rex?

Long distance!

• • • • •

How can you tell if a clock is hungry?

It'll go back for seconds!

• • • • •

What do baby ghosts wear?

Pillowcases!

• • • • •

Why did the school nurse run away?

To catch a cold.

• • • • •

Why are wizards good at fishing?

Because they really know how to cast a spell!

• • • • •

Why did Mickey Mouse shrink himself?

So he could be with Minnie!

• • • • •

What is a tree's favorite state?

Oak-lahoma!

What do snakes put on their kitchen floors?

Rep-tiles.

• • • • •

What type of snake does a baby play with?

A rattlesnake!

• • • • •

What do you call a bug with four wheels and a trunk?

A Volkswagen Beetle.

• • • • •

Why do witches fly on brooms?

Because vacuum cleaners are too heavy!

• • • • •

Why is a calendar so popular?

Because it has a lot of dates!

• • • • •

Why was Cinderella bad at soccer?

Because she ran away from the ball.

• • • • •

What do you call a whale band?

An orca-stra!

• • • • •

What do you call little bugs that live on the moon?

Luna ticks!

• • • • •

Why did John walk backwards to school?

It was back to school day!

• • • • •

Who can jump higher than a 10-story building?

Anybody! Buildings can't jump.

• • • • •

What did the rabbit give his girlfriend?

A 14 carrot ring!

• • • • •

What do you call a worm in a fur coat?

A caterpillar!

• • • • •

Which object is king of the classroom?

The ruler!

• • • • •

Where do doctors go on vacation?

Ill-inois!

• • • • •

Why can Mount Everest hear everything you say?

Because it's covered with mountaineers!

• • • • •

Why did the lady spray her clock?

Because it had ticks!

• • • • •

Which side of a bird has the most feathers?

The outside!

• • • • •

Why don't ducks tell jokes when they fly?

Because they would quack up!

• • • • •

Which subject did the witch get an A+ in?

Spell-ing.

• • • • •

What is a soldier's favorite fish?

Swordfish!

• • • • •

What is Dracula's favorite landmark?

The Vampire State Building!

• • • • •

What did one girl firefly say to the other?

You glow girl!

• • • • •

How do you make a whale float?

Get a huge glass, a can of soda, 2 coops of ice cream and a whale!

• • • • •

Why did the robber wear blue gloves?

Because he didn't want to get caught red-handed.

• • • • •

What do you call a cow with a twitch?

Beef jerky!

• • • • •

What do you wear on the beach?

Sand-als!

• • • • •

Why didn't anyone want to sleep with daddy dinosaur?

Because he was a Bronto-snore-us!

• • • • •

What's green, slimy and hangs in trees?

Giraffe snot!

• • • • •

How come the dalmation couldn't hide?

Because he was already spotted.

• • • • •

How do you make cool music?

Put your CD's in the fridge!

• • • • •

Why did the boy ask his dad to come to school?

To take a Pop quiz.

• • • • •

Why would Snow White make a good judge?

Because she's the fairest of them all!

• • • • •

Why did the boy sleep with a ruler?

Because he wanted to check how long he slept!

• • • • •

What's a cheerleader's favorite drink?

Root beer!

• • • • •

Why can't a bicycle stand up?

Because it's two tired!

• • • • •

What did the religious skunk say?

Let us spray!

• • • • •

What has a tail and a head but no body?

A coin!

• • • • •

What do you call a grizzly bear with no teeth?

A gummy bear.

• • • • •

What did the banana say to the doctor?

I'm not peeling very well!

• • • • •

Where did the ship go when it was sick?

It went to see a dock!

• • • • •

What did one plate say to the other plate?

Food's on me tonight!

• • • • •

How do you stop a werewolf howling in the back of a car?

Put him in the front!

• • • • •

I have 52 legs, 27 arms, 775 eyes and 500 ears. What am I?

A liar!

• • • • •

What is a scarecrow's favorite fruit?

Straw-berries!

• • • • •

What do smart birds like to study?

Owl-gebra!

• • • • •

What has forty feet and sings?

The school choir.

• • • • •

What do you call a cow in the backyard?

A lawn moo-er!

• • • • •

What did the summer say to the spring?

Help! I'm going to fall!

• • • • •

What kind of horse only comes out at Halloween?

A nightmare!

• • • • •

Why did the farmer buy a brown cow?

Because he wanted chocolate milk!

• • • • •

What can you break by saying its name?

Silence.

• • • • •

Why was the computer injured?

Because it slipped a disk!

• • • • •

Do you want to hear the joke about the bed?

Sorry, it hasn't been made yet.

• • • • •

Why didn't the quarter roll down the hill with the nickel?

Because the quarter had more cents.

• • • • •

What's a pirate's favorite restaurant?

Arrrr-by's!

• • • • •

What animal is always ready to travel?

An elephant, as it has a trunk!

• • • • •

What goes 99 clunk, 99 clunk?

A centipede with a wooden leg.

• • • • •

Why did the boy swallow three dollar bills?

Because it was his lunch money!

• • • • •

What do you call a sick dog?

A Germy Shepherd!

• • • • •

Where do American cows come from?

Moo York!

• • • • •

What's a mummy's favorite type of music?

Rap music!

• • • • •

What do ants take when they're sick?

Ant-ibiotics!

• • • • •

Who is a cow's favorite heroine?

Moo-lan!

• • • • •

How did the burger propose?

With an onion ring!

• • • • •

Did you hear the one about the spaceship?

It was out of this world!

• • • • •

What did one eye say to the other?

Don't look now, but something between us smells!

———————

• • • • •

Why are most baseball games held at night?

Because the bats sleep during the day.

• • • • •

Why did the boy take a bale of hay to bed?

To feed his night-mare!

• • • • •

What did sushi A say to sushi B?

Wasabi?

• • • • •

What do runners do when they forget something?

They jog their memory!

• • • • •

What is a pirate's favorite planet?

Maaarrrs!

• • • • •

What did the plate say to the spoon?

Dinner's on me!

• • • • •

Why did Mickey Mouse go into space?

He was trying to find Pluto!

• • • • •

How long does it take a gymnast to get to class?

A split second.

• • • • •

What do you get when 354 blueberries try to get through a door at the same time?

Blueberry jam!

• • • • •

What did one volcano say to the other volcano?

I lava you!

• • • • •

What do you wash a phone with?

Dial!

• • • • •

What do witches ask for at hotels?

Broom service!

• • • • •

How do dogs get rid of fleas?

They start from scratch!

KNOCK-KNOCK JOKES

Knock knock,
Who's there?
Cash
Cash who?
No thanks, but I would like a peanut instead!

• • • • •

Knock knock,
Who's there?
Banana
Banana who?
Knock knock,
Who's there?
Banana
Banana who?
Knock knock,
Who's there?
Orange,
Orange who?
Orange you glad I didn't say banana!

• • • • •

Knock knock,
Who's there?
Honey bee,
Honey bee who?
Honey bee a dear and get me a drink!

● ● ● ● ●

Knock, knock
Who's there?
Cows go
Cows go who?
No, cows go MOO!

• • • • •

Knock, knock
Who's there?
Lettuce
Lettuce who?
Lettuce in, it's cold out here.

• • • • •

Knock, knock
Who's there?
Ya
Ya Who?
Nah mate, I prefer Google

• • • • •

Why did Sally fall off the swing?
Because she had no arms.

Knock knock,
Who's there?
Not Sally.

• • • • •

Knock, knock
Who's there?
Daisy
Daisy who?
Daisy me rollin', they hatin'

• • • • •

Knock, knock
Who's there?
Idunnop
I dunnop who?
Ha ha, you done a poo!

• • • • •

Will you remember me in an hour?
Yes
Will you remember me in a day?
Yes
Will you remember me in a week?
Yes
Will you remember me in a year?
Yes
I don't believe you.
Knock, knock
Who's there?

• • • • •

Knock, knock
Who's there?
Shelby
Shelby who?
Shelby coming round the mountain, when she comes!

• • • • •

Knock, knock
Who's there?
Art
Art who?
R2D2

• • • • •

Knock, knock
Who's there?
Broccoli
Broccoli who?
Broccoli doesn't have a last name, silly!

• • • • •

Knock, knock
Who's there?
Olive
Olive who?
Olive you

• • • • •

Knock, knock
Who's there?
Atch
Atch who?
Bless who!

• • • • •

Knock knock,
Who's there?
Howie
Howie who?
I'm fine, how are you?

• • • • •

Knock, knock
Who's there?
Lena
Lena who?
Lena a little closer and I'll tell you

• • • • •

Knock, knock
Who's there?
Eddy
Eddy who?
Eddybody home?

• • • • •

Knock, knock
Who's there?
Jamaica
Jamaica who?
Jamaica mistake?

• • • • •

Knock, knock
Who's there?
Eva
Eva who?
Eva you're deaf or the doorbell isn't working

• • • • •

Knock, knock
Who's there?
Heaven
Heaven who?
Heaven seen you in ages!

• • • • •

Knock, knock
Who's there?
Spell
Spell who?
W-H-O

• • • • •

Knock, knock
Who's there?
Mikey
Mikey who?
Mikey doesn't fit in the hole

• • • • •

Knock, knock
Who's there?
Nana
Nana who?
Nana your business!

• • • • •

Knock, knock
Who's there?
Justin
Justin who?
Justin the neighborhood, thought I would drop by.

• • • • •

Knock, knock
Who's there?
Luke.
Luke who?
Luke through the the peep hole and find out!

• • • • •

Knock, knock
Who's there?
Europe
Europe who?
No I'm not, you're a poo!

• • • • •

Knock, knock
Who's there?
Says
Says who?
Says me, that's who.

• • • • •

Knock, knock
Who's there?
Ann
Ann who?
Ann Easter bunny
Knock, knock
Who's there?
Anna
Anna who?
Anna other Easter bunny.
Knock, knock
Who's there?
Maura
Maura who?
Maura Easter bunnies.
Knock, knock
Who's there?
Howie
Howie who?
Howie going to get rid of these Easter bunnies?

• • • • •

Knock, knock
Who's there?
Woo
Woo who?
Don't get so excited, it's just a joke!

• • • • •

Knock, knock
Who's there?
Interrupting cow.
Interrup....
-MOOOOOOOOOOOOOOO!!

• • • • •

Knock, knock
Who's there?
Oink oink.
Oink oink who?
Make up your mind, are you a pig or an owl?!

• • • • •

Knock, knock
Who's there?
Wendy
Wendy who?
Wendy wind blows, the cradle will rock

• • • • •

Knock, knock
Who's there?
Tank
Tank who?
You're welcome!

• • • • •

Knock, knock
Who's there?
Chimney
Chimney who?
Chimney cricket, have you seen Pinocchio?

• • • • •

Knock, knock
Who's there?
A little old lady
A little old lady who?
I didn't know you could yodel!

• • • • •

Knock, knock
Who's there?
Oliver
Oliver who?
Oliver across the road from you!

• • • • •

Knock, knock
Who's there?
Frank!
Frank who?
Frank you for being my friend!

• • • • •

Knock, knock
Who's there?
Wooden shoe!
Wooden shoe who?
Wooden shoe like to hear another joke?

• • • • •

Knock, knock
Who's there?
Beets!
Beets who?
Beets me!

• • • • •

Knock, knock
Who's there?
Howard!
Howard who?
Howard I know?

• • • • •

Knock, knock
Who's there?
Dishes
Dishes who?
Dishes a really bad joke!

• • • • •

Knock, knock
Who's there?
Leaf
Leaf who?
Leaf me alone!

• • • • •

Knock, knock
Who's there?
Stopwatch
Stopwatch who?
Stopwatch you're doing and let me in!

• • • • •

Knock, knock
Who's there?
Cash
Cash who?
I knew you were nuts!

• • • • •

Knock, knock
Who's there?
Adair
Adair who?
Adair once but now I'm bald!

• • • • •

Knock, knock
Who's there?
Arfur
Arfur who?
Arfur got!

• • • • •

Knock, knock
Who's there?
Nanna
Nanna who?
Nanna your business!

• • • • •

Knock, knock
Who's there?
Henrietta.
Henrietta who?
Henrietta worm that was in his apple.

• • • • •

Knock, knock
Who's there?
Iva
Iva who?
I've a sore hand from knocking!

• • • • •

Knock, knock
Who's there?
Orange
Orange who?
Orange you going to let me in?

• • • • •

Knock, knock
Who's there?
King Tut
King Tut who?
King Tut-ey fried chicken!

• • • • •

Knock, knock
Who's there?
Ben
Ben who?
Ben knocking For 10 minutes.

• • • • •

Knock, knock
Who's there?
I am
I am who?
You mean you don't know who you are?

• • • • •

Knock, knock
Who's there?
Cook
Cook who?
Hey! Who are you calling cuckoo?

• • • • •

Knock, knock
Who's there?
Sadie.
Sadie who?
Sadie magic word and watch me disappear!

• • • • •

Knock, knock
Who's there?
Abbot
Abbot who?
Abbot you don't know who this is!

• • • • •

Knock, knock
Who's there?
Two knee
Two knee who?
Two-knee fish!

• • • • •

Knock, knock.
Who's there?
Roach
Roach who?
Roach you a letter, did you get it?

• • • • •

Knock, knock
Who's there?
Dozen
Dozen who?
Dozen anybody want to let me in?

• • • • •

Knock, knock
Who's there?
Toby
Toby Who?
Toby or not Toby, that is the question.

• • • • •

Knock, Knock
Who's there?
Police
Police who?
Police stop telling these awful knock, knock
jokes!

• • • • •

Knock Knock
Who's There?
Nunya
Nunya Who?
Nunya Business

• • • • •

Knock Knock
Who's There?
Jesus
Jesus Who?
How many do you know?

• • • • •

Knock knock
Who's there?
Nobel
Nobel who?
No bell so i'll knock.

• • • • •

Knock, knock
Who's There?
Ben
Ben who?
Ben knocking on the door all afternoon!

• • • • •

Knock, Knock
Who's there?
Panther
Panther who?
My panther falling down!

• • • • •

Knock, knock
Who's there?
Pig
Pig who?
Pig up your feet before you twip!

• • • • •

Knock, knock
Who's there?
Hippo
Hippo who?
Hippo birthday to you, hippo birthday to you!

• • • • •

Knock, knock
Who's there?
Ben
Ben who?
Ben knocking at your door for a while!

• • • • •

Knock, knock
Who's there?
Carl
Carl who?
Carl back when there's somebody in!

• • • • •

Knock, knock
Who's there?
Cow
Cow who?
Cow you doing?

• • • • •

Knock, knock
Who's there?
Annie
Annie who?
Annie body home?

• • • • •

Knock, knock
Who's there?
Britney Spears

Britney Spears who?
Knock, knock
Who's there?
Oops, I did it again!

• • • • •

Knock, knock
Who's there?
A herd
A herd who?
A herd you were home so I came over

• • • • •

Knock, knock
Who's there?
Alison
Alison who?
Alison wonderland is a great book!

• • • • •

Knock, knock
Who's there?
Amayan
Amayan who?
Amayan the way?

• • • • •

Knock, knock
Who's there?
Annapolis
Annapolis who?
Annapolis is a fruit

• • • • •

Knock, knock
Who's there?
Lettuce
Lettuce who?
Lettuce pray

• • • • •

Knock, knock
Who's there?
Snow
Snow who?
Snow business like show business

• • • • •

Knock, knock
Who's there?
Joanna
Joanna who?
Joanna come out and play?

• • • • •

Knock, knock
Who's there?
Nobel
Nobel who?
Nobel, that's why I knocked!

• • • • •

Knock, knock
Who's there?
Vonda
Vonda who?
Vonda hear some more knock knock jokes?

• • • • •

Knock, knock
Who's there?
Ida
Ida who?
Ida rather you didn't knock on my door this time
of night

• • • • •

Knock, knock
Who's there?
Joe
Joe who?
Joe mama

• • • • •

Knock, knock
Who's there?
Stan
Stan who?
Stan back, I'm going to knock down the door!

• • • • •

Knock, knock
Who's there?
Dwayne
Dwayne who?
Dwayne the bathtub, I'm dwowning

• • • • •

Knock, knock
Who's there?
Says
Says who?
Says me, that's who!

• • • • •

Knock, knock
Who's there?
Baby bee
Baby bee who?
Baby bee a doll and bring me a snack

• • • • •

Knock, knock
Who's there?
Barbie
Barbie who?
Barbie cue chicken!

• • • • •

Knock, knock
Who's there?
Figs
Figs who?
Figs the doorbell, it's broken!

• • • • •

Knock, knock
Who's there?
Olive
Olive who?
Olive next door to you

• • • • •

Knock, knock
Who's there?
Turnip
Turnip who?
Turnip the volume, it's too quiet!

• • • • •

Knock, knock
Who's there?
Water
Water who?
Water you doing in my house?

• • • • •

Knock, knock
Who's there?
Apple
Apple who?
Apple your hair

• • • • •

Knock, knock
Who's there?
Car
Car who?
Car go beep beep

• • • • •

Knock, knock
Who's there?
The
The who?
The postman

• • • • •

Knock, knock
Who's there?
Radio
Radio who?
Radio or not, here I come!

• • • • •

Knock, knock
Who's there?
Ima
Ima who?
Ima going to tickle you!

• • • • •

Knock, knock
Who's there?
Gorilla
Gorilla who?
Gorilla me a cheese sandwich!

• • • • •

Knock, knock
Who's there?
Amy
Amy who?
Amy fraid I've forgotten!

• • • • •

Knock, knock
Who's there?
Doris
Doris who?
Doris locked, that's why I'm knocking!

YO MAMA JOKES

Yo Mama is so fat that her belly button gets home 15 minutes before she does

• • • • •

Yo mama is so fat that when she talks to herself, it's a long distance call

• • • • •

Yo mama is so fat that people jog around her for exercise

• • • • •

Yo mama is so fat that she walked into the Gap and filled it

• • • • •

Yo mama is so fat that her cereal bowl came with a lifeguard

• • • • •

Yo mama is so fat that she doesn't eat with a fork, she eats with a forklift.

• • • • •

Yo mama is so fat that when she sits around the house, she sits AROUND the house.

• • • • •

Yo mama is so fat that she had to go to Seaworld to get baptized.

• • • • •

Yo mama is so fat that she could sell shade.

• • • • •

Yo mama is so fat that when she runs the fifty-yard dash she needs an overnight bag.

• • • • •

Yo mama is so fat that she's on both sides of the family.

• • • • •

Yo mama is so fat that we're in her right now.

• • • • •

Yo mama is so fat that she went to the movies and sat next to everyone.

• • • • •

Yo mama is so fat she's got her own area code.

• • • • •

Yo mama is so fat she's in two time zones.

• • • • •

Yo mama is so fat that when she gets in an elevator it has to go down.

• • • • •

Yo mama is so fat that she left the house in heels and came back in flip flops.

• • • • •

Yo mama is so fat that you have to grease the door and hold a twinkie on the other side to get her out the door.

• • • • •

Yo mama is so fat that when she lies on the beach, Greenpeace show up and try to tow her back into the ocean.

• • • • •

Yo mama is so fat that the National Weather Service names each of her farts.

• • • • •

Yo mama is so fat that when she calls herself it's a long distance call.

• • • • •

Yo mama is so fat that when she sits on an iPod it turns into an iPad.

• • • • •

Yo mama is so fat that when she sings, it's over for everybody.

• • • • •

Yo mama is so fat that she fell in love and broke it.

• • • • •

Yo mama is so fat that she was born on the fourth, fifth and sixth of June.

• • • • •

Yo mama is so fat that when she turns around people throw her a 'Welcome Back' party.

• • • • •

Yo mama is so fat she has to iron her pants on the driveway.

• • • • •

Yo mama is so fat when she breaks her leg, gravy comes out.

• • • • •

Yo mama is so fat that when she goes to a buffet they have to install speed bumps.

• • • • •

Yo mama is so fat when she trips on 4th avenue, she lands on 12th

• • • • •

Yo mama is so ugly when she entered the ugly contest they said, 'sorry, no professionals'

• • • • •

Yo mama is so ugly when the Terminator said 'I'll be back', he left running

• • • • •

Yo mama is so ugly her pillow cries at night

• • • • •

Yo mama is so ugly her shadow quit

• • • • •

Yo mama is so ugly people go as her for Halloween

• • • • •

Yo mama is so ugly she has seven years bad luck just trying to look at herself in the mirror

• • • • •

Yo mama is so ugly she makes onions cry

• • • • •

Yo mama is so ugly she hurts my feelings

• • • • •

Yo mama is so ugly your dad first met her at the pound

• • • • •

Yo mama is so ugly she has to creep up on water to get a drink

• • • • •

Yo mama is so ugly she has to trick-or-treat over the phone

• • • • •

Yo mama is so ugly she has a sign in the yard that says 'beware of dog'

• • • • •

Yo mama is so ugly that she gave Freddy Kruger nightmares

• • • • •

Yo mama is so ugly they changed Halloween to 'yomama-ween'

• • • • •

Yo mama is so ugly Hello Kitty said goodbye to her

• • • • •

Yo mama is so ugly when she walks into the bank they turn off the security cameras

• • • • •

Yo mama is so ugly not even Santa would let her sit on his lap

• • • • •

Yo mama is so ugly she went into a haunted house and came out with a paycheque

• • • • •

Yo mama is so ugly she got arrested for mooning when she took the bag off her head

• • • • •

Yo mama is so ugly she made a Happy Meal cry

• • • • •

Yo mama is so dumb she spent 20 minutes looking at an orange juice carton because it said 'concentrate'

• • • • •

Yo mama is so dumb she got fired from the M&M factory for throwing away the W's

• • • • •

Yo mama is so dumb that she got hit by a parked car

• • • • •

Yo mama is so dumb she put a quarter in a parking meter and waited for a gumball to come out

• • • • •

Yo mama is so dumb she sold her car for gas money

• • • • •

Yo mama is so dumb she got locked in a mattress world and slept on the floor

• • • • •

Yo mama is so dumb when I said drinks are on the house, she went and fetched a ladder

• • • • •

Yo mama is so dumb she duuuuumb

• • • • •

Yo mama is so dumb she failed a survey

• • • • •

Yo mama is so dumb she gave birth to you

• • • • •

Yo mama is so dumb she stopped at a stop sign and waited all day for it to say go

• • • • •

Yo mama is so dumb she returned a donut complaining there was a hole in it

• • • • •

Yo mama is so dumb she tried to trade in brownie points at a cake sale

• • • • •

Yo mama is so dumb I told her to buy a color TV and she said, 'what color?'

• • • • •

Yo mama is so dumb when a robber stole her TV she ran after him saying 'you forgot the remote!'

• • • • •

Yo mama is so dumb she crashed into McDonalds because the sign said 'drive-thru'

• • • • •

Yo mama is so dumb when she hears about a serial killer she hides the Cheerios

• • • • •

Yo mama is so dumb she bought tickets to XBox Live

• • • • •

Yo mama is so dumb she looked in the mirror and said 'stop copying me!'

• • • • •

Yo mama is so dumb she dialed 911 on the microwave

• • • • •

Yo mama is so dumb when dad said it's chilly outside she brought a spoon and a bowl

• • • • •

Yo mama is so dumb she tried to drown a fish

• • • • •

Yo mama is so dumb she took a spoon to the Super Bowl

• • • • •

Yo mama is so dumb she tripped over a cordless phone

• • • • •

Yo mama is so hairy if she could fly she'd look like a flying carpet

• • • • •

Yo mama is so hairy they filmed 'Gorillas in the Mist' in her shower.

• • • • •

Yo mama is so hairy Bigfoot took a picture of her.

• • • • •

Yo mama is so hairy she has dreadlocks on her back.

• • • • •

Yo mama is so hairy she shaved and she disappeared.

• • • • •

Yo mama is so hairy you almost died of rugburn at birth.

• • • • •

Yo mama is so hairy she's a stunt double for Chewbacca in Star Wars.

• • • • •

Yo mama is so hairy she got a trim and lost 10 pounds.

• • • • •

Yo mama is so hairy she shaves her legs with a weed wacker.

• • • • •

Yo mama is so hairy she can go to Antarctica and not get cold.

• • • • •

Yo mama is so hairy she got cornrows on her feet.

• • • • •

Yo mama is so hairy that for Halloween she dies herself green and goes as a bush.

• • • • •

Yo mama is so hairy she went into a store and the clerk said, 'no pets allowed'.

• • • • •

Yo mama is so hairy she could be sold as a Chia pet.

• • • • •

Yo mama is so hairy when she went to the Empire State Building people shouted 'King Kong!'

• • • • •

Yo mama is so hairy when she went to the zoo, the monkeys whistled at her as she walked past.

• • • • •

Yo mama is so old she delivered Jesus.

• • • • •

Yo mama is so old that when she was in school there was no history class.

• • • • •

Yo mama is so old she said, who's Oprah?

• • • • •

Yo mama is so old her memory is in black and white.

• • • • •

Yo mama is so old she planted the first tree at Central Park.

• • • • •

Yo mama is so old when she farts dust comes out.

• • • • •

Yo mama is so old she knew Burger King when he was a prince.

• • • • •

Yo mama is so old she drove a chariot to high school.

• • • • •

Yo mama is so old Jurassic Park brought back memories.

• • • • •

Yo mama is so old the key on Benjamin Franklin's kite was to her apartment.

• • • • •

Yo mama is so old she used to babysit for Yoda.

• • • • •

Yo mama is so old she was a waitress at the Last Supper.

• • • • •

Yo mama is so old her birth certificate says 'expired' on it.

• • • • •

Yo mama is so old her birth certificate is written in Roman numerals.

• • • • •

Yo mama is so old she DJ'ed at the Boston Tea Party.

• • • • •

Yo mama is so old she took her driver's test on a dinosaur.

• • • • •

Yo mama is so old her social security number is 1.

• • • • •

Yo mama is so old the back of her head looks like a raisin.

• • • • •

Yo mama is so old when she was born the Dead Sea was just getting sick.

• • • • •

Yo mama is so old when she was told to act her own age, she died.

And that's all, folks! We hope you laughed your way through this book and will have jokes you can share with your friends for many years to come.

We would very much appreciate your review on Amazon — it helps us to make bigger and better books next time!

If you'd like more joke books, search 'Jenny Kellett' on Amazon to find my author page.

Printed in Great Britain
by Amazon